*An
Empty
Pot's
Darkness*

José Angel Araguz

An
Empty
Pot's
Darkness

A book of Octaves

Airlie Press
PORTLAND
OREGON
2019

Airlie Press is supported by book sales, by contributions to
the press from its supporters, and by the work donated by all
the poet-editors of the press.

P.O. BOX 82653
PORTLAND OR 97282
WWW.AIRLIEPRESS.ORG

EMAIL: EDITORS@AIRLIEPRESS.ORG

Cover Art: "Moth Urn" by Ani Schreiber
Book Design: Beth C. Ford, Glib Communications & Design

First Edition
ISBN: 978-1-950404-02-5
Library of Congress Control Number: 2019947570
Printed in the United States of America

CONTENTS

I [was]...impressed with the contention of the late T'ang poets that most things worth saying could be said within eight lines...

—Jim Harrison, "A Natural History of Some Poems"

OCTAVES OF YOUTH

The fable where the man has to go

fifteen years without a bath or shave

and wear a bearskin, whose pockets held

gold in endless supply, followed me

long into adolescence: stubble

began to hide my face, and the air

around me seemed repellant: I'd reach

into my skin for gold, pull out words.

The porch with missing steps gives the house
a broken mouth look. Grass rises through
the gaps, bleaches to the yellow-white
the past is made from. Memory grows

      until it can't be seen. This house
      falls apart upon itself, grins
      absentmindedly at the end
      of the block, as the light leaves it.

I walk the T-Heads and hear water
    plash and turn upon itself.
    The wind is wide and braver
here. I feel it run along my hands.

Anyone would think me idle, false,
    or whatever words I call
    myself half-thinking, halfway
to where the sun sinks and turns to sound.

Birds have their ways of building nests:

a foraging, a collecting,

  a leaving and coming back.

When they pass the cemetery,

they must wonder what is built here.

  How do I expect to live

in a home made up of words? All

  I collect here is silence.

You can see their faces covered
in dust, gone unseen until now.
  The clouds shift outside,

and light falls across the picture
frame, the glass goes from flash back to
  dust-covered faces,

  collected, waiting,
  specks until recalled.

The moon you are describing is the one you are creating
– William Stafford

How many moons between us, friend?
I meet you under circumstances
bad and good: bad, because you're not here,
good, because I get to listen

and hear the moon you'd have me see.
Moon of my own efforts: where to start?
My questions? What are questions? Tonight,
the moon is in the shape of one.

Enough drinks, you'll see me smile at
the devil. You'd think I just stared
at the wall, listened as it held court,
clucking my tongue, blowing smoke, waving

a cigarette in quick triangles.
That's what I play in this symphony.
An idle sound, a lie, really,
but we play the part we're given.

FOR DENNIS FLINN

Promise me you'll never put me in
a story. I unfold these words from
others said over ten years and wish

    they'd lead to more. Advice. Jokes.
    Living will in your wallet.
    When you took it out and wrote

my name alongside your wish to be
cremated, the page creased like your face.

My room in your house was bare.

I painted the walls bright green
for no other reason than
it made you laugh. Living there,
I'd hear you turn and shuffle
papers, until I couldn't.

The day you died: I didn't
know it until days later.

You gave me a door to make a desk,
    set it across cinderblocks,
a door between the floor and ceiling.

I began to write. I'd knock sometimes
    when stuck, the echo short, but
enough for me to want to listen.

Did you write this on the door? I still see
you hold the page as if you could walk through.

Never told me not to put you in the earth.

I have dreams where you are soil and stone.
I go to speak, grit cuts at my mouth,
white and gray dust, the color of moths
at your screen door the year you kept me
off the streets and writing in your house.

I just did what anyone would do, you'd say,
through the white and gray dust of your beard.

You lived without power like a
grudge, lit lamps as others puzzled. This is just
how one lives. The nights I lived there, I stumbled
   in the dark and wrote my poems by
   the light of a kerosene lamp.

When the light gave out, I would write by the moon.
When the moon gave out, I'd write trusting the words
   would still be there in the morning.

You spent afternoons in your armchair,
in and out of sleep. You'd call my name
to see if I was around. Evenings,
you'd go housesit, leaving me the dark.

Since you died in someone else's house,
no one's explained it to your armchair:
He is sleeping in another life.
When he wakes, you'll know it when you creak.

One night, a friend began to
kick and spit against another car
after locking her keys in hers. You
    yelled her name until she stopped.

She asked us to stay, moved cat litter
    so I could sleep on her couch.
Some have it nice, you said. *We have poems.*
We're the diversity they speak of.

No plot then, no arc, no denouement.

The day you turned ash, I wasn't there.
I can only tell it like you might
through white, gray words: *You rest in pieces.*
Perhaps you'd laugh. *You merely left scraps.*
A chuckle. A crackle in your throat.
You left life as broke as you had lived.

I can almost hear your armchair creak.

The snow today brings back the first snow,
    white like this, at turns pristine,
    then bitter like this, broken
by steps whose depths can't be guessed like this.

We've treated one another like snow,
    watched each other fall and drift.
    You have come today like snow,
and made me pause. And like snow you leave.

OCTAVES FOR O

la luz descalza sobre el mar y la tierra dormidos [1]

O, let's go walking then, like

the light across the ocean,

and the light across the land.

No one will hear us. Pages

in a book rest with a light,

you saw it once. I am here

to tell you it remains. Light,

O, dances, barefoot, soundless.

---

[1] These syllabic octaves were written by riffing off end lines from poems by Octavio Paz ("O"). This first comes from "Domingo en la isla de Elefanta" (line translation: *the light barefoot over the sleeping sea and land*).

de la piedra / abierta por la mirada [2]

That is the feeling that came:

the story of your visit

to the famous poet who

made you wait: You saw him mark

out words, scribble more, again

mark. You asked why. He said to

make the automatic more

automatic. O, I see—

---

[2] "Piedra Blanca y Negra" (*line translation: of the stone / opened by the gaze*).

mis palabras se volvieron visibles un instante 3

Joseph Cornell has us beat:
we look in fascinated,
faces made water for a
moment, water that reflects
meaning, not thought but a light
past thought, glimmer, and glint of
what is found. O, what did you
find? O, the box shuts us out.

―――――――――――

3 "Objectos y Apariciones" (line translation: *my words
became visible for a moment*).

sobre la hoja de papel / el poema se hace / como el día /

sobre la palma del espacio [4]

Could we write: *morning, window,*

light—and write: *afternoon stretched,*

and so on—Write past things missed

by the eye, missed by being

alive—Write: *the tree outside*—

the feeling of lines moving

past you—Write: *the paper wind*

moves—O, we'd miss the missing.

---

[4] "El Fuego de Cada Día" (line translation: *across the sheet of paper / the poem is made / like the day / across the palm of space*).

La realidad es más real en blanco y negro [5]

Paper, again: poet, ink.

What you would say on paper

to paper: What you would say,

ink, again. Poet: pebbles

of breath, until the breath is

paper. Still paper, again,

in the hands. Poet, you ink

too fast: Paper, still your hands.

------

[5] "Cara al Tiempo" (line translation: *reality is more real in black and white*).

la alegria / de los vivos / es la pena de los muertos [6]

Pity, my reality:

To dance while dust dithers, drums

softly. Is that you rising

as I thumb your Collected,

pace the room to stay awake—

Important, the dust, the dance

from black, white, and back again.

Is that you: paper laughing—

---

[6] "Epitafio de una Vieja" (line translation: *the joy / of the living / is the pain / of the dead*).

el corazón del agua...el cielo anda en la tierra [7]

Heart of the water, you write,

your hand like mine, earthbrown, kept

on wrestling with daybreak,

that time itself a battle.

Color over color break

the sky over the earth of

my hand. O, here the sky you

saw keeps walking in each heart.

---

[7] "Madrugada al Raso" (line translation: *heart of the water...heaven walks on earth*).

estoy / en el espacio / etcetera [8]

O, the vine, the kind that turns

itself through, around fences:

were you to try to follow,

leaf to leaf, the light would rise,

turn in its own way, you would

forget where you started, which

leaf—this leaf, perhaps—and on,

turning through, around your words.

---

[8] "Reversible" (line translation: *I am / in space / etcetera*).

desmemoria me guía / hacia el reverse de la vida [9]

O, what will be forgotten

last: words, stray hair on the neck,

where the water glass was placed,

the pitcher's weight in your hand

before, after, the water's

push on glass, clear as nothing,

push on itself, nothing clear

except the now: which now last—

[9] "A Través" (line translation: *amnesia guides me / to the reverse of life*).

FOR LA LLORONA

I saw her in Corpus Christi,
  no river, only skin,

another's ring on her finger,
  the gold lost in the dark.

She said seventeen should leave town,
  and never speak of this.

  What's there to speak of? We
had stars for light, so little light.

She told me she loved my hands once
    as I played my guitar.

Awaiting her call each evening,
    I sat as the moon passed.

I sat til I forgot my name,
    and who I answered to.

    In its case, a forced chord
sounds now, whenever a door slams.

I met her first in songs about
    children, sirens, and loss.

I have lived in many cities,
    but always the same stars

shifting slightly, her face shifting
    across a bottle's side.

    What hand stopped writing our
lyrics, and what hand writes these days?

I've tried and failed to speak of her,
    speaking only her name,

even then, only a whisper,
    pencil scratch about stars.

El que tiene amor tiene
    pena writes the siren

    in song, love followed by
what could be pain, sorrow, pity.

Each day passes by as she passed,
    becomes a yesterday.

I wrote of her blue dress early,
    mistook it for the sea.

Yesterdays follow like shadows;
    the past's night, and won't give.

    I wrote of a blue that
left me breaking against myself.

What makes a boy chase after love,
  and what makes a man run?

Her daughters were my age and lost
  when we spoke in secret,

lost in the river of our skin,
  faces unclear even now.

I chased her not knowing
a thing; left knowing even less.

I answered her call one evening,
   her husband barked my name.

I answered her call one evening,
   her husband barked my shame.

Palm trees I used to write under,
   keep hands open tonight.

   I offer these words up
as alms to be spent on the wind.

FOR CHRISTINE MALOY

The poet died. The words keep coming,
fill pages in someone else's book.
The weather keeps changing in the sky.
I know there are no last words, just words
that last, or don't. The words keep changing.
Mosquitoes. Palm trees. Wind changes each.
Each moves when you move away. You left
pages turned in a South Texas sky.

On Facebook, people still seek you out.

    This last face, pixelated,

    thumbnail hitchhiking to now,

gives a grin, lends small glints to your eyes,

constellates them to sharp points of light.

    Is this the shape of your myth?

    A held look, a look away

    I cannot triangulate.

We shared a stage, took turns not talking,
listened, still as lamps lining the streets.

Spotlight in a small café: even
    the moths would hold still. The lines
of poems, like the lines of their bodies,
    would move when we moved. Nervous,
we seemed lost, sifting paper for sound.

Paper-white, the moon is blank tonight.

Not enough laughter could be
anybody's epitaph. You shared
    good news the last time we spoke.
    With you, it wasn't always
good. From others, I heard a rotten
    lover, failing health, and poems.

I made you laugh once, small talk before
you performed: my words, nothing new, gone.

Faces made while reading: who keeps them?

As a child, I read before mirrors,
and never caught myself. Later, when
I watched you read, your eyes would look out
from the stage, down to where the words were
falling. We couldn't see each other.

Each face is a page read only to
read one's self: in mine, I read your loss.

Family Reports First Known Death in
Nueces County Related to Flu—
because, at thirty-four, you were out
of statistical range, you would be
irretrievable but for the air
behind your name, the news anchor's voice
announcing you have gone, and these words
now, the other side of where you are.

I watched the clip only once,

your photo spliced in and out of shots

of hospital rooms, doctors talking

    not of you but of people

    not receiving shots, a voice

not saying your name said everyone

is at risk, your face, everyone, spliced

    into the closing comments.

In words you cannot read, others come,

attempt revelatory phrasing,

    say *miss, loss,* say *you* and *thanks.*

I know those words. From the look you give,

I know my face could be any face.

    When the lights on the screen change,

    Your face remains unchanged.

    This page won't tell me more.

OCTAVES OF EXPERIENCE

The rings inside trees are made by gods
who contemplate and walk in circles.
    The years are marked with their footsteps,
    silence. Fate: that we can only

see the rings by chopping down the tree.
That, when we do, we see only age,
    history and purpose patterned
    like one cursed to stone in stories.

I learn the Chinese word for world
is a compound, heaven and earth,
and think how you can see them both:
see clouds and sky, see rocks and dirt.

The hell I know collects in thoughts
of flame and what I should not want,
but goes unseen. Unchained like this,
my hell compounds to words, to worlds.

The parade of colors marching through
her hair fell white. Next fell laughter, then
conversation altogether. Then,
(always *then*) she'd fall right through herself.

Had she her wish, there'd be a cup
with something of her days in it.
She'd look right through the fallen light,
she'd look all night, then drink it up.

April was a different color
before her eyes appeared in the rain:
falling, parting eyes, eyes set to pass.
That color came around, clung to

the grass, filled pools on my walk home,
my clothes became heavy with her eyes.
When I undressed to change, my skin felt
cool, charged, as if lingered upon.

My heart has a pasta's stickiness,

    like when it's thrown against

    the wall to see if cooked.

A throw, a splay, a fall: not ready.

The smell of salt and wine on love's skin.

    A throw, a tug, a give;

    steady, but never right.

An empty pot's darkness come morning.

*AN EMPTY POT'S
TESTAMENT*

I was born in the eighth month of

nineteen eighty-two, a year with

an eight in the not-quite-middle.

Already things were uneven

by being even; four numbers

means no middle, means if cut in

half, my birth year would be empty

space, absence, really, nothing here.

Now that I have erased myself,

I can begin: Memories of

Matamoros merge with those of

Corpus Christi, each stretch of four

syllables vital to my life,

to explaining where I come from,

eight syllables hanging on air;

when I speak them, nothing matters.

The nothing I am in language—
this my roots and origins; lost,
any exactness of the word
José. It means another man,
another presence signified
in another city and life
where he lived so far from where I
live now; yet here my father now.

I hear my mother clearer in

memories of when we shared rooms

from Leopard to Navigation

to garage apartments to where

she lives still now on Ramsey Street.

Our voices travelled, argued, wore

the other down until one left—

in stanzas now, echoes sounding.

In Italian, "la stanza" means
"room." In Spanish, it's "cuarto." Move
one letter over, you have four
(*cuarto, cuatro*) like a heartbeat,
the 'r' takes turns being part of
a place, then concept—What I mean
is the rooms I sat silent in

when young, pen in hand—what's held here?

Around the lion starves the young.

Around a fever starves the heart.

Around my twenties lions paced,

my heart starved the young man I was.

It felt fever my heart favored.

It felt lion's teeth grazed my breath.

My breath passed where no food paced, young

lion pacing where no cage was.

When I was wasting away, hands
were moving to fill in the space
with words—that I couldn't talk then
but talk now—lungs like pockets
I keep rummaging through, holding
up a turn of phrase—*just try me*—
hear it give over to *just tie
me*—float away to *just dying*—

In my thirties, I'm just joking
until I'm not—after my death
my favorite clothes will grow cold like
a room everyone cleared out of,
my favorite words will grow careless,
push past others on their way out,
my fondness for counting out each
syllable will be left behind.

To grass I leave behind sunlight.

To sunlight I leave behind rain.

To rain I leave behind your name.

To your name I leave behind peace.

To peace I leave behind my scars.

To scars I leave behind healing.

To healing I leave behind wounds.

To wounds I leave behind pulsing.

When I felt my pulsing leave me
in the emergency room—when
I bled out and was nothing but
the pain of each breath, and the fear
in between—when Cincinnati
seemed the last city I'd write in,
my wife found herself praying, found
words to break the silence I caused.

I have wanted to say something
of my living, which is dying,
which is a shoelace's tightness
in each step, which is moving on,
which is a metaphor, which is
what one finds in writing, which is
what I do when not living how
others see fit, which is the end.

ACKNOWLEGMENTS

The poems in "for Dennis Flinn" "for Christine Maloy" and "Octaves of Youth" were previously published in the chapbook *Corpus Christi Octaves* (Flutter Press, 2014). Thank you to Sandy Benitez for giving these poems an early home.

The poems in "for La Llorona" loosely interpolate details from the folksongs about the Mexican folktale La Llorona (the weeping woman) with details from a personal relationship.

The following poems from "Octaves of Experience" were published in *The Inflectionist Review*: "Snow falls with the same sound as her words" "April was a different color" and "I learn the Chinese word for world."

The poems in "Octaves for O" were previously published in the anthology *desde Hong Kong: Poets in Conversation with Octavio Paz* (Chameleon Press Ltd, 2014). Thanks to editors Germán Muñoz, Tammy Ho, and Juan José Morales for providing an early home to this tribute.

Special thanks to John Drury and Daniel Groves for their insight and help with some of the early drafts of these sequences. Thanks also to Sam Roderick Roxas-Chua for allowing me to read from this project at *The Poetry Loft* early in its making. Special thanks as well to Brian Clifton for friendship and poetic insight. And one last thanks to the editors of Airlie Press for working with me on this project.

ABOUT THE PUBLISHER

Airlie Press is run by writers. A nonprofit publishing collective, the press is dedicated to producing beautiful and compelling books of poetry. Its mission is to offer a shared-work publishing alternative for writers working in the Pacific Northwest. Airlie Press is supported by book sales and donations. All funds return to the press for the creation of new books of poetry.

COLOPHON

The titles are set in Adobe Caslon Pro Italic. The poems are set in Stickley, created by designer Michael Stickly, a humanist, oldstyle type font with a contemporary execution and subtle, elegant variations in proportion, detail, and contrast.